Pine Ridge Reservation: Yesterday & Today

by

Greg Gagnon

and

Karen White Eyes

Original photographs by
Ellen Gagnon

BADLANDS NATURAL HISTORY ASSOCIATION
Interior, South Dakota

Acknowledgements

This work was partially supported by the South Dakota Council for the Humanities. The authors wish to express their gratitude for that support. All opinions and interpretations presented are solely those of the authors.

PINE RIDGE RESERVATION: YESTERDAY & TODAY

 For information, write Badlands Natural History Association, P.O. Box 6, Interior, South Dakota 57750.

First Edition: August, 1992
First Printing: August, 1992
Second Printing: May, 1999

Library of Congress Cataloging-in-Publication Data

Gagnon, Gregory and Karen White Eyes
Pine Ridge Reservation: Yesterday & Today

iv + 34 p.
Bibliography: 2 p.
Includes 17 photographs, 2 maps

International Standard Book Number 0-912410-13-2

Cover photos: On Pine Ridge Reservation, many Lakota live comfortably with their traditional culture and the trappings of modern technological society.

CONTENTS

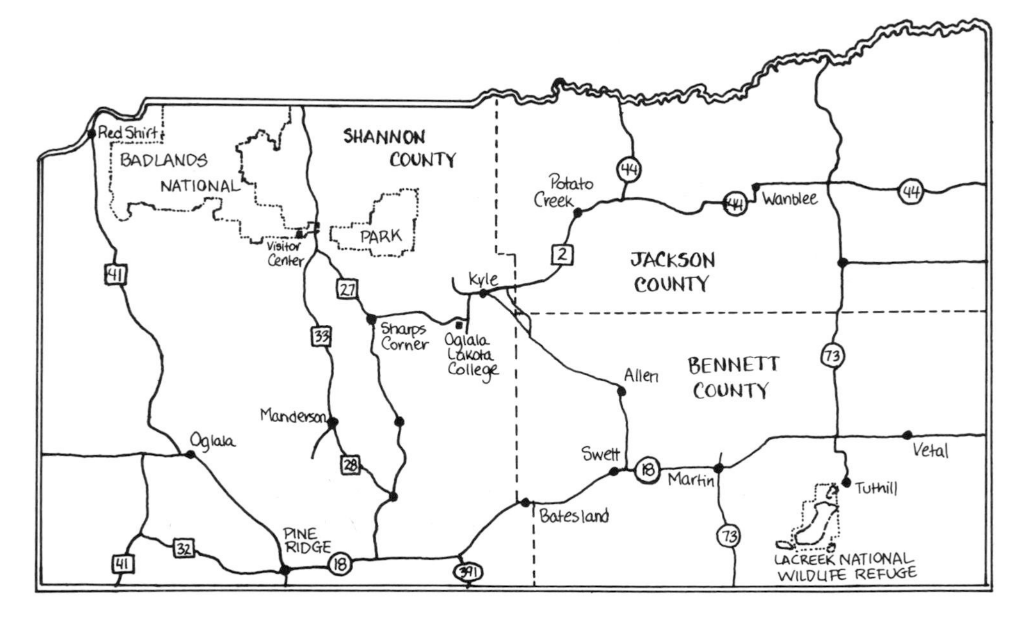

Pine Ridge Reservation and its associated communities. Illustration by Sophie Cayless.

AN ENDURING PEOPLE

This brief introduction to Pine Ridge Reservation- home of the Oglala Lakota- demonstrates several realities. The Oglala people and their culture have not disappeared with the buffalo. Indeed there are more Oglala people living on the reservation today than in 1878 when the reservation was created.

The Oglala have always borrowed technology, ideas, and institutions from other peoples while maintaining the integrity of their society. Development of the Plains culture with technology from Europeans and ideas from other

Adam Espinosa fleshes a deer hide at the 1991 Wazi Paha Festival, Kyle, South Dakota.

Indian nations is one example of adaptability. The current tribal government with its stress on decentralized, consensus-based decision making within the context of a multi-million dollar constitutional government is another. Even the revival of organizations designed to provide self-help, like the Gray Eagle Society, demonstrates the use of cultural tradition to attack modern problems. Some changes were forced on the Oglala while others were embraced. All, however, received an Oglala twist.

Anyone driving through the reservation today can see this blending of Lakota and non-Lakota– traditional dancers who work on computers, village residents who live in modern air-conditioned homes, blond pow-wow dancers, tribal police who manage softball teams, and Ph.D.s who set up tipis. All of these scenes and people represent Pine Ridge Reservation and Oglala Lakota culture.

PINE RIDGE RESERVATION

Pine Ridge Reservation is the second largest in the United States. Its 5,000 square miles are located within the boundaries of southwestern South Dakota. Congress created the reservation in 1889 from land collectively owned by the Sioux tribes before the Louisiana Purchase. The current reservation is but a tiny remnant of much larger land holdings guaranteed the Sioux by earlier treaties. The Sioux tribes did not wish to sell their land and had resisted the 1889 land cession approved by Congress as they had resisted earlier "forced takings." The United States government pledged to provide educational and economic assistance as payment for the land taken for as long as the Sioux tribes needed assistance.

The 1889 Congressional act that created Pine Ridge Reservation for the Oglala tribe of the Sioux nation created other reservations within South Dakota too. Standing Rock, Crow Creek, Lower Brule, Cheyenne River, and Rosebud Reservations are now the homelands of various Lakota-speaking tribes. Histories of these reservations, particularly the adjacent Rosebud Reservation, are intricately intertwined with the history of the Oglala. As on all reservations, the Pine Ridge tribal government is not a branch of state government. It exists as a remnant of a formerly independent sovereign state recognized by the United States.

Approximately 19,000 people live on Pine Ridge Reservation. About 16,000 Oglala tribal members reside there with non-Indians and members of other tribes and reservations. Another 6,000 Oglala live throughout the United States. Only enrolled members of the Oglala Sioux tribe participate as reservation citizens and are subject to the jurisdiction of the tribal government. Congress has eliminated Indian jurisdiction over non-Indians leaving them subject to federal jurisdiction. Oglalas fall under tribal law for most civil matters and misdemeanors, but Indian felony cases are tried in federal

Pine Ridge Reservation– a landscape dominated by rolling grasslands, scattered stands of ponderosa pine, and stark, eroded badlands– is home to the Oglala Lakota.

courts. Two portions of Pine Ridge Reservation– Bennett and Jackson Counties– are subject to South Dakota state laws, except on trust land. These examples merely hint at the legal confusions of reservation life.

Tribal government derives its legitimacy from the 1936 constitution granted to the Oglala by the federal Indian Reorganization Act. Most Oglala contend that Pine Ridge is a sovereign nation (like Canada or Mexico) and has never surrendered its sovereignty to the United States or any other government. Sovereignty and jurisdictional disagreements provide a constant source of friction among Pine Ridge, the state of South Dakota, and the United States.

The Oglala Sioux Tribal Council has sixteen elected members representing nine electoral districts: Pine Ridge Village, Eagle Nest, La Creek, Medicine Root, Pass Creek, Porcupine, Wakpamni, White Clay, and Wounded Knee. These districts are located within Shannon County and portions of Jackson and Bennett counties. The tribal president is elected at large, as is the vice president, while the tribal council chooses other executive council members. All serve two year terms. Tribal courts adjudicate the full range of civil cases and misdemeanors. Judges are chosen by the tribal council. Numerous agencies and services, similar to those in most American communities, fall under the control of the tribal government. The tribe operates more than twenty departments and has chartered the Oglala Lakota College.

District governments are analogous to county governments in the United States although they have fewer independent powers. These nine district governments recognize fifty-one traditional communities whose primary purpose is to channel community opinion to district government and the tribal council. This system of community representation is a deliberate adaptation of traditional government centered on small bands or communities called *tiyospaye.*

Several characteristics of Pine Ridge and all reservations confuse many people unfamiliar with reservation life. The first is what is termed trust responsibility. Through numerous court decisions, executive orders and acts of Congress, the United States has recognized that tribal governments and American Indians are like wards, and the national government is like a trustee. This means that tribal land and resources are protected by the federal government as its responsibility. The federal agency charged with administering Native American programs is the Bureau of Indian Affairs (BIA). Many feel that the BIA has not been an effective trustee.

Second, treaties and agreements between the tribes and the United States government describe the special responsibilities of the federal government toward Indian nations in recompense for the surrender of Indian lands. Congress and the executive branch have developed uniform legislation and programs for financing federal responsibilities to Pine Ridge and other reservations. Some of the compensation for surrendered land takes the form of services. For instance, the federal government provides funding for education, medical treatment, roads, and even college funds for some students.

The Oglala and other Indians do not receive monthly checks from the government. This myth probably originated from a misunderstanding about the lease checks that Indian land owners receive from the Bureau of Indian Affairs. The Bureau acts as leasing agent for most Indian-owned land on the reservation. Indians are eligible for the financial assistance provided for all Americans such as Aid to Families with Dependent Children (AFDC), food stamps, and farm subsidies.

Pine Ridge Reservation is one of the most poverty-stricken areas of the United States. Shannon County, located entirely within the reservation, has one of the lowest per capita incomes in America. In almost one-third of Pine Ridge households no one has a job. Individual household income averages around $3,000 annually for the entire reservation. Unemployment hovers at 80% according to tribal government figures.

Despite the obvious problems of living on the reservation, the Oglala people cling to their country because it is the only place where they can be Oglala instead of "just an Indian" or "just another minority" in the larger American society. Although the employment opportunities are limited, the Oglala are rooted culturally on Pine Ridge Reservation, and most would not migrate from their country.

Since time immemorial, the Oglala Lakota have demonstrated a resilience and an ability to change that has allowed them to survive as a fluid, evolving society. The ancestors of Pine Ridge's population adapted horses and guns to their needs; they adapted to the fur trade; and they adapted to reservation life controlled by the federal government. Now they are adapting to self-determination. During their history as a people, the Oglala have maintained a culture begun in the misty past, and they have added not only new technology, but also different people and new ideas from the world at large.

TRADITIONAL ORIGINS AND CULTURE

Once there was only one people. Dakota/Nakota/Lakota, as they called themselves, meant "friends...allies...to be friendly." This nomadic people once roamed the plains and prairies of North America east to Wisconsin, north into Canada, west to the Bighorn Mountains of Wyoming, and south to Nebraska, Kansas, and Colorado. Tribal traditions hold that long ago they originated in the Black Hills and received instructions on how to live from White Buffalo Calf Woman. She brought the Sacred Calf Pipe and reinforced the traditional male values of bravery, generosity, fortitude, and wisdom. To females, she added the values of truthfulness and child bearing. Seven sacred ceremonies served the people: the Sweat Lodge, the Vision Quest, the Sundance, the Making of Relatives, Tossing of the Ball, the Buffalo Ceremony, and the Keeping of the Spirit/Soul. All of these ceremonies except the Tossing of the Ball and the Buffalo Ceremony are observed on Pine Ridge Reservation today. Their religion encompassed and governed all aspects of their everyday lives- government, health, education, migration, hunts, and even warfare. These ceremonies and their place in Lakota culture are complex. Readers who wish to learn more about them should consult studies cited in the bibliography.

The Lakota belonged to the *Oceti Sakowin*, or Council of Seven Fires. The Oceti Sakowin corresponds to those people who, today, are commonly called "the Sioux." At an early time, the Sioux began to evolve into three main groups, each speaking a different dialect of the same language. The Dakota were the largest and were considered to be the mother group. They had four sub-groups represented in the Oceti Sakowin. The Nakota had two sub-groups in the Oceti Sakowin, and the Lakota only one. Winter counts, traditional historical records, suggest that strife within the Oceti Sakowin occurred long ago. This may have corresponded with a rise in power and influence of the Lakota who diverged from the main group.

The Dakota, also called the Santee, remained east of the Mississippi in Minnesota; the Nakota, or Yanktonai, left the Dakota to live on the prairies of southeastern South Dakota; and the Lakota, also known as the Teton, moved west of the Missouri River.

The Lakota became the largest subdivision of the Sioux. They developed the Plains culture after receiving the horse in the seventeenth century. The Lakota subdivided into seven bands: Oglala, Sicangu, Hunkpapa, Miniconjous, Sihasapa, Itazipacola, and Oohenupa. Members of these bands (later declared tribes by the federal government) considered themselves related historically, culturally and linguistically. After the reservations were established, Lakota were forced to enroll in one tribe or another. Pine Ridge Reservation is the home of the Oglala. Today, the Oglala recognize that their ancestors came from several different tribes (including the Cheyenne) as recently as the turn of the century. However, all enrolled members are Oglala, regardless of their actual Indian ancestry, including "mixed bloods" who combine European and Indian genes.

Traditional Lakota government revolved around the tiyospaye- a band or village comprised of relatives, extended family, and other followers. Leaders of tiyospaye were individuals who had proven themselves through their virtuous lives, their intelligence, their outstanding ability to protect the tiyospaye, and their knowledge of the values and ways of their people. Laws were essentially those of tradition. Needless to say this system was a fluid arrangement. Tiyospaye leaders gravitated to other leaders and eventually a group of tiyospaye became a tribe, like the Oglala. A few tribal leaders dominated the tribe's major decisions (war, peace, range of territory) and occasionally met with other tribal leaders.

It is important to realize that centralized decision-making was not part of Lakota political culture. Group decision-making based on respect for the individual's right to choose remains a vital concern in Oglala life. This was democracy based on individual rights tempered by custom, and should not be confused with the constitutional democracy of the United States.

The basis of the Lakota culture was the buffalo, or *tatanka*. All parts of the buffalo were used to make a wide variety of goods useful in everyday life, and it formed a staple of the Lakota diet. Buffalo has recently been found to be high in protein, low in fat and cholesterol, and, generally, much healthier than meat from beef cattle. Buffalo meat was eaten fresh, or it was commonly preserved by drying. Dried buffalo was called *papa*, and it is similar to jerky.

Buffalo meat was supplemented with *tinpsila-* wild turnips, *canpa-* chokecherries, *kanta-* plums, and other wild and domesticated fruits and vegetables. Chokecherries were also preserved for later use during the winter by pounding and drying them. A mixture of the papa was pounded to a fine powdery texture and mixed with the ground chokecherries and a little animal fat. This was called *wasna* and was taken by young men on long journeys or war parties. It was also used during ceremonies and is still used today.

Some of the domesticated vegetables were corn and squash. These too were dried for later winter consumption. Dried corn was called *wastunkala* and, when mixed with papa, made a very tasty soup. Domesticated vegetables were acquired in trade with the Arikara and Mandan, agricultural tribes with whom the Lakota had frequent contact.

OGLALA HISTORY: PRE-RESERVATION DAYS

Although the Lewis and Clark Expedition first contacted a people called the Oglala near present-day Pierre, South Dakota, the Oglala and other Lakota tribes ranged throughout the Great Plains north of the Platte River. The Oglala were on the western edge of a continuous Lakota expansion and were part of an extensive trade network centered on the Mandan-Hidatsa towns along the Missouri River. By 1795, a few Spanish and French merchants operating from St. Louis began trading with this network.

Fur traders are intimately related to the history of the Oglala. After the Louisiana Purchase, several St. Louis-based companies established trading posts throughout the West to take advantage of an already existing Indian trade network. The first trading posts in Lakota territory were built along the Missouri River. The Lakota saw these posts as beneficial since they provided them with a source of trade items.

During this time, the Oglala and other Lakota tribes continued to increase their hegemony over a wider territory. By 1834, Lakota territory included most of present-day North and South Dakota and extended westward to the Bighorn Mountains and southward to the Platte River. The Lakota ranged even beyond this vast area. They were the largest, most successful military force on the high plains. They acquired this territory at the expense of the Shoshone, Crow, Arapahoe, Arikara, Cheyenne, Pawnee, and Ponca nations.

In 1834 two separate developments determined the future of the Oglala. The majority of the Oglala tiyospaye came under the domination of Bull Bear, with a smaller number directed by Smoke. Each group had consolidated many of their cultural and other community activities near present-day Bear Butte State Park in western South Dakota. Oglala traditions describe this area as a crucial site in the practice of traditional Vision Quests and annual Sun Dances. Bear Butte, as a descriptive term, incorporates an area extending west to Devil's Tower. The Cheyenne nation considers the Bear Butte region as the geographic location of their origins, a consideration reinforced by Oglala tradition.

The Oglala political situation in 1834 is unclear, but they may have been in the process of consolidating their loosely governed bands into a single tribal organization under one or two dominant leaders. Clearly, Bull Bear and Smoke combined numerous tiyospaye under their leadership. Aside from the spiritual base the Bear Butte area provided, the Oglala needed a base that would allow access to the southern buffalo herds, the most numerous on the High Plains and a source of the manufactured items upon which their power and their lifestyle depended.

The area at the confluence of the North Platte and Laramie rivers offered potential as a new center of Oglala activity and had the additional advantage of being an area where Oglala warriors had established hegemony. To retain control of the area, the Oglala needed a source of guns and other trade goods.

Simultaneously, fur trading companies were pushing toward the western mountains along well worn Indian travel routes that followed the Platte across central Nebraska. William Sublette realized that the junction of the North Platte and Laramie rivers, where numerous Indian nations had camped and traded for generations, was an ideal point for a trading post. He foresaw that the fur trade would soon concentrate on buffalo hides as beaver were trapped out. He built Fort William, later renamed Fort Laramie, hoping to trade with several Indian tribes and the mountain men. Sublette sent messengers north to encourage the Oglala to trade at Fort Laramie. Their trade would allow him to compete with the larger American Fur Company.

Bull Bear moved about 4,000 Oglala to the vicinity of Ft. Laramie, and established the locus of Oglala activity for the next forty years. Smoke's band followed within the year. Ironically, Sublette sold out to the American Fur

Company, and the Oglala drove all other tribes from the new center of the Oglala empire.

Fort Laramie became the center of Oglala economic and political life. The American Fur Company provided access to imported goods and an outlet for Oglala products. Eventually, all of the Oglala tiyospaye spent more and more time in the area, and it was from Fort Laramie that the Oglala domi-

Fort William, later renamed Fort Laramie, was a focal point of Lakota history and economic life in the early 1800s. National Park Service photo.

nated their portion of the Lakota territory, disciplined invaders, and lived the life romanticized by the film, "Dances With Wolves."

The American Fur Company introduced new bloodlines to Oglala ancestry in the Fort Laramie area. "Frenchmen" and "Squawmen," as they were called by nineteenth century travellers, made up the backbone of the fur trade. These French-descended Americans were a legacy of France's colonial efforts near St. Louis. With nearly a century of experience in the Indian fur trade, they were obvious recruits for the American Fur Company. James Bordeaux managed Ft. Laramie and directed the activities of traders named Richard, Janis, Pourier, Bissonette, and Garnier, among others.

These young men married Lakota women and became quasi-Oglala themselves. Their "half-breed" children were members of the tribe. This group of mixed ancestry remains important today and has always been a major factor in Oglala history. They served as interpreters, distributors of goods, and warriors. In reservation days, the mixed-bloods were often the ones who made the easiest adaptation to the American presence and policies. Red Cloud had roughly 100 mixed-blood relatives by 1878; Crazy Horse married a mixed-blood; most twentieth century tribal presidents have been mixed-blood.

Although Ft. Laramie was an Oglala community, other Lakota tribes often stayed in this area. Many Brule, who now occupy Rosebud Reservation, moved to Ft. Laramie by the 1860's. Typically the males left for war, and whole tiyospaye ranged in all directions for hunting. Despite the mobility of Oglala life, some Oglala could always be found at Ft. Laramie.

The brief period from 1834 to 1849 was the best of all times for the Oglala. They had a large territory; they were feared by their enemies; they were free and sovereign lords of the plains. Unfortunately, the tides of history flowed over the Oglala and engulfed the fur traders as well.

Ft. Laramie became a major rest stop along the Oregon Trail. Buffalo began to disappear, victims of a wanton slaughter by whites. As thousands of migrating Americans poured into Oglala country, Oglala leaders considered what responses were best for their nation- a problem faced by small nations throughout history. Americans demanded protection of their "right" to cross and hunt in Oglala country whenever they wanted and felt that Oglala land belonged to the United States. The Oglala and the rest of the Lakota nation disagreed.

In 1849, the United States government purchased Ft. Laramie from the American Fur Company and moved in troops. Two years later, the United States negotiated a series of Ft. Laramie treaties with the Lakota, Cheyenne, Arapahoe, Assiniboines, Shoshoni, Arikara and Crow. These agreements delineated the extent of Oglala and other tribal territories. The Indian nations agreed to allow passage across their territory in return for specified payment to the tribes. These treaties recognized Oglala conquests of the previous fifty years and clearly described Lakota territory as embracing a vast region including much of eastern Wyoming and western South Dakota.

Ensuing years saw the beleaguered Oglala responding to the invasion of miners, the never-ending stream of emigrants along the Oregon Trail, and the creation of an unauthorized series of fortresses on the Bozeman Trail. "Red Cloud's War" of 1866-68 was a Lakota response to the invasion of their land. Although Red Cloud, an Oglala, was a dominant leader, he was only one of several prominent Lakota who distinguished themselves during the war. Among others were Young Man Afraid of His Horses, American Horse and the young front-line leader, Crazy Horse. In 1866, Captain William J. Fetterman lost eighty men, killed by Lakota warriors near Ft. Phil Kearny in what the losers called a massacre.

Red Cloud's War ended in 1868 with a second Ft. Laramie Treaty. This treaty is the basis for nearly all of the conflict today between Oglala Lakota and Americans. In the treaty, the United States recognized the western half of South Dakota as the Great Sioux Reservation and the Oglala heartland of eastern Wyoming as "unceded Indian territory." It guaranteed that no Americans would ever be allowed into this region except under specific provisions such as trade and government business. The United States abandoned the Bozeman Trail forts and agreed to pay the Indians annuities, provide an agent to represent the government, furnish education and training to the Indians, and protect Indian land. Perhaps the key provision was Article XII. This article guaranteed that the terms of the treaty could not be changed nor any land ceded "unless executed and signed by at least three-fourths of all the adult male Indians." The Oglala contend today that no territorial changes, including the taking of the Black Hills in 1877, are legal according to the Treaty of 1868 until three-fourths of the Indian males agree. Even the United States' attorneys have conceded that this has never happened.

Between 1868 and 1873 the Oglala remained near their power center at Ft. Laramie, although events elsewhere continued to influence them. The westward expansion of America continued, and the formerly dominant Oglala found themselves pressured in their own country by settlements, miners, and the U.S. military. Annunities replaced trade for the most part, and compliant traders were superceded by army commanders. The Oglala received constant admonitions from Indian agents who represented the new power in their homeland.

Moreover, the buffalo were disappearing, hunting grounds were overrun by settlers, and eventually gold was discovered in the Black Hills of South Dakota. The U.S. Army and the Indian Department pressured the Oglala to relocate to the newly constructed Fort Robinson, Nebraska. The buffalo were nearly gone, the fur trade was merely a memory, and the Indian Department controlled the annuities. Many Oglala acquiesced, and together with their

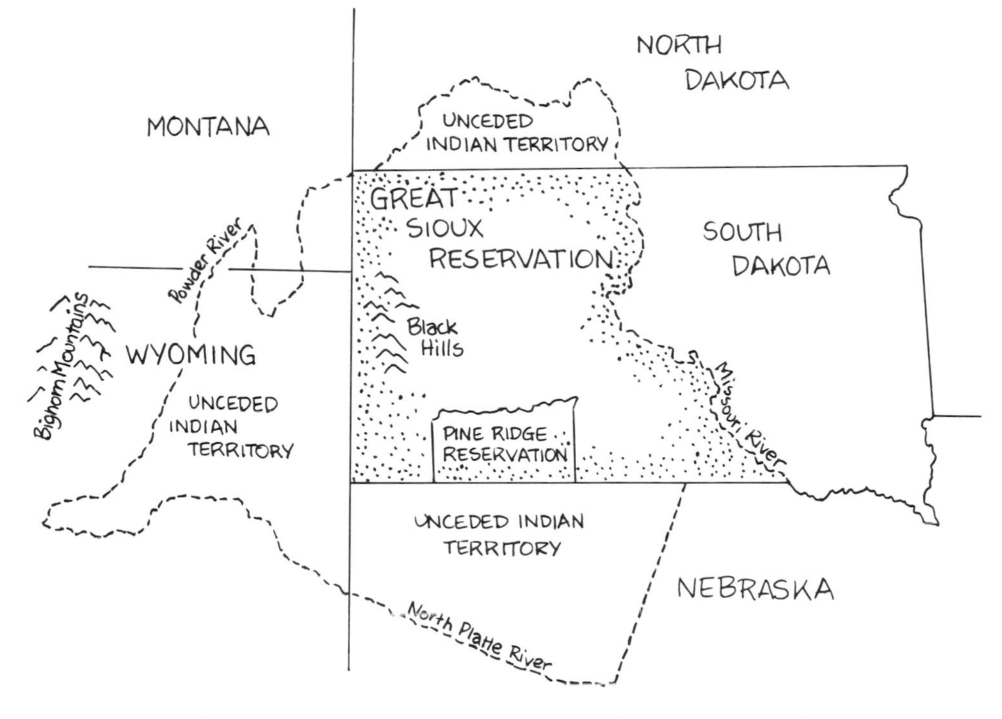

Sioux Territory as delineated in the 1868 treaty ending Red Cloud's War. Illustration by Sophie Cayless.

famous leader, Red Cloud, they moved to Fort Robinson in 1873 to begin a life of increasing domination by the Americans and by policies created in Washington, D.C.

However some Oglala did not move to Fort Robinson. They remained on their land in the Black Hills and in eastern Wyoming and Montana where they tried to maintain their freedom. In 1874 an Army expedition led by Lieutenant Colonel George Custer confirmed that abundant gold existed in the Black Hills. The United States attempted to buy the Black Hills. After the Oglala Lakota refused to sell, the Army ordered all Indians to return to their agencies- Fort Robinson for the Oglala. Crazy Horse, American Horse

Eliza Morrison, star quilt maker, at the Kyle fair.

Pow-wow shade near Kyle. Dance
observers sit under the brush.

Counselor and student. Devona Whirlwind Horse and Freida Poor Bear in LaCreek District

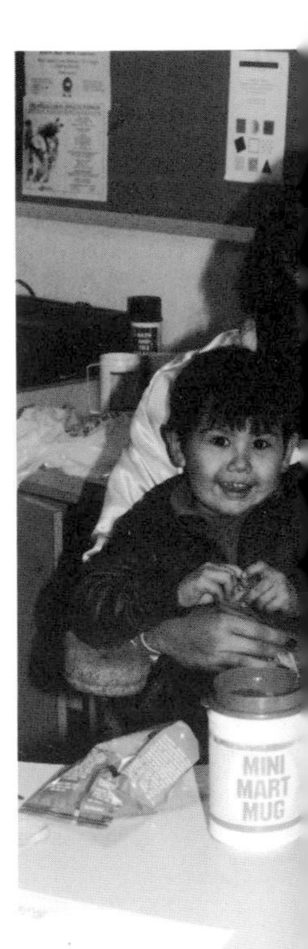

Cathy Iron Cloud and h
the babysitter does not sh

m in the circle center while

Ron Du Bray, Oglala Sioux Tribal Police. Sergeant Du Bray works in Pass Creek District.

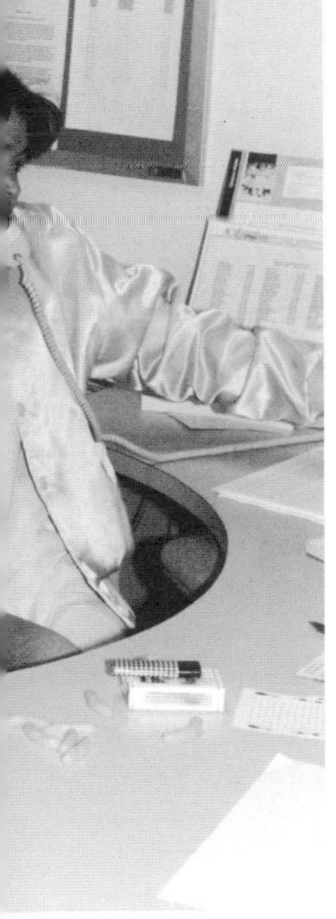

Kyle Pourier. Sometimes

Headstart students in Kyle II, Medicine Root District. Each district has at least one Headstart center.

and other Oglala did not move. Troops were assembled to force these "renegades" and "hostiles" onto the agencies.

These orders were issued despite the provisions of the Fort Laramie Treaty which confirmed the right of the Lakota to hunt and live in these "unceded lands." When the Lakota did not return to Fort Robinson, the U.S. Army moved to force their return.

In late spring of 1876, an expedition under the command of Brigadier General Crook was halted by Crazy Horse's army at the Rosebud. The Lakota army then returned to the Little Big Horn. Custer ended a career marked by recklessness on June 25 when he attacked the combined army of the Lakota, Cheyenne, and Arapahoe.

The victory at the Little Big Horn remains an important psychological event in Indian-American history. However, it marked the end of the Oglala as a military force able to defend their country. Within a year Crazy Horse was dead and all of the Oglala were concentrated at Fort Robinson.

Although military resistance was over, the Oglala leadership clung tenaciously to their homelands. In 1877, most of the Oglala Lakota leaders, threatened by withdrawal of their annuities, reluctantly agreed to sign the 1877 Agreement which took the Black Hills. Importantly, considerably less than the required three-quarters of adult Lakota signed this new "agreement" even though they were threatened with starvation. Red Cloud, American Horse the Younger, Little Wound, Lone Man, and other Oglala leaders managed to keep the government from forcing the Oglala to move all the way to the Missouri River. By 1878, Pine Ridge Reservation was established at its present location. Subsequent "agreements" forced upon the Lakota divided the remnants of the Great Sioux Reservation to allow colonization of South Dakota by immigrant farmers and miners.

After the reservation was created, the American government began its assault on Lakota culture. The intention was to make farmers of the Lakota. This would require the Lakota to change their religion, their concept of property, and their educational system.

The beleaguered Oglala and the other Lakota people continued to resist their subjugation in a number of ways. The most famous form of resistance was the Ghost Dance.

THE LAKOTA AND THE GHOST DANCE

In times of extreme crisis, many Indian nations looked to religious solutions, and prophets arose to lead the people. Wovoka, a Paiute, became the prophet for the Plains Indians.

He dreamed that Indians should dance the Ghost Dance in order to encourage God to remove the Americans, revive their dead ancestors, and bring back the buffalo. Oglala leaders, including Short Bull, visited Wovoka and returned to the Lakota reservations with the necessary ceremonies while adding Lakota interpretations and artifacts such as the idea that a Ghost Shirt would turn American bullets from its wearer.

By 1890, the Lakota and several other Plains Indian tribes were Ghost Dancing by the hundreds to drive the white men away, not by war, but by

Wounded Knee, location of the 1890 massacre and the 1973 confrontation. It is under consideration for designation as a National Memorial. Heritage Museum collection.

divine intervention. Predictably, some Indian agents and American settlers in Indian country panicked. They called upon the federal government to stop what they saw as preparation for war. The Ghost Dance was outlawed, and agents called upon the military to suppress it. Sitting Bull, a spiritual leader, was killed by Indian police at the Standing Rock Reservation. His death led to wholesale fear among the Lakota who expected the Army to arrest or kill the nearly helpless Lakota. Large numbers of people including Big Foot and his band fled to Pine Ridge Reservation for safety. Big Foot and his tiyospaye were intercepted by the Seventh Cavalry near the community of Porcupine. They were told to camp along Wounded Knee Creek while the soldiers formed an armed cordon around them. When the Army attempted to disarm the Lakota, shots were fired, and the soldiers began a heavy fusillade that killed hundreds of helpless Lakota, many of the them the elderly, women, and children. Within a few days after the Wounded Knee Massacre, the last hostilities between the Lakota and the United States ended with the surrender of the remaining Ghost Dancers.

Clearly, the Oglala had to accommodate to domination by the United States. Accommodation was, after 1890, the only choice. The degree to which the Oglala would accommodate, even in institutions such as schools, where assimilation was enforced, remained an open question.

THE PATTERN OF RESERVATION LIFE: 1878 - 1960

After the United States eliminated the Oglala as a military threat, the government and "Friends of the Indian" began a process of Americanization. Christianity was purveyed on all reservations, and missionaries spearheaded an assault on the core of Lakota culture. Late nineteenth century Americans assumed that their religion was best for Indians and that Indian religion was, at best, ignorance and, at worst, devil worship. Missionary activity on Pine Ridge Reservation had been granted to the Episcopal Church by the government and until 1881, no other sects were allowed to proselytize. This was part of a policy to prevent Christian churches from competing with one another on each reservation. Part and parcel of the Christian assault was the Bureau of Indian Affairs' education system. At first, a few Oglala children

Holy Rosary Mission, site of Red Cloud Indian School, in the 1940's. Heritage Museum collection.

were sent to boarding schools like those in Carlisle, Pennsylvania, Hampton, Virginia, and Genoa, Nebraska. Here uniformed Indian children were taught that their parents were heathen savages, that Indians could only do vocational work, and that Christianity was good. Oglala parents resisted by hiding their children, but many were caught and sent away. Some Indian parents decided to cooperate in the hope that their children would be adapted to the new world. A number of parents sent their children to Holy Rosary and Pine Ridge boarding schools so the children could eat three meals daily and live comfortably while their parents sought work in Nebraska and South Dakota.

On Pine Ridge the first mission school was the Catholic Holy Rosary Mission. Many Oglala graduated from Holy Rosary, and some became tribal and national leaders. Holy Rosary exemplifies some of the changes in reservation life. Holy Rosary Mission School is now named Red Cloud School. It now encourages Oglala language and culture whereas, prior to the 1960's, Catholic Oglala were taught to suppress their culture. Red Cloud School's Heritage Museum has an excellent Native American art collection.

The first Bureau of Indian Affairs school was in Pine Ridge Village, and it too pressed for the destruction of Oglala language and culture. The Bureau's school now teaches Lakota culture and has an all-Oglala, elected school board. Considerable change has occurred since the times when weeping Oglala parents watched their children's hair being cut to a "civilized" length.

Despite this direct assault, Oglala culture persisted. Ceremonies were held way out in the districts where, inexplicably, the Oglala police could not find them. Somehow children kept arriving at school speaking Lakota. The agents of civilization were even co-opted. Several of the Episcopal priests were either Dakota or Lakota like Vine DeLoria and Chris Whipple. The Presbyterian church sent Sam Weston, a Dakota, and Dennis Gilbert, an Oglala, to several reservation parishes. Although these Indian ministers firmly believed in Christianity, they did modify the ferocity of Christian dogma to allow for Oglala language and customs. Of course, legalized polygyny (a Lakota custom of non-binding marriage) disappeared to be replaced by serial cohabitation. Officially, married women began using their husband's surnames.

These efforts to undermine the validity of Oglala culture and language have been resisted by many so the culture has survived. However, great damage was done. Many Oglala lost their language, and many accepted the message that theirs was an inferior culture. Many Oglala did their best to assimilate into the dominant Anglo-American culture.

Traditional government officially disappeared. Bureau of Indian Affairs agents simply overruled traditional leadership and hired "progressive" Oglala to enforce BIA laws. Bureau "Boss Farmers" were assigned to each of the reservation districts as agents of assimilation who were to make "their Indians" into farmers. Traditional living and governing patterns were disrupted by the Allotment Act of 1887. This act was designed to give the head of each Oglala household 160 acres. Any unallotted land was to be opened for non-Indian homesteaders. Most of Bennett and Jackson counties were allotted, and today the majority of land in both counties along with significant portions of Shannon County are owned by non-Indians. These areas are not considered part of the reservation by the federal and state governments. Many Oglala lost their land because they did not understand the concept of land as a commodity that could be bought, sold, and taxed. Some Oglala did make the adjustment and profited from allotment. In Bennett County, Oglala allotees helped organize the county under state government.

New Indian farmers were given a plow, a horse team, wagon, and seeds. Contests in garden production were sponsored by the Boss Farmers, and fairs were held to demonstrate "civilized" sewing and farm products. The Oglala turned these 4-H style fairs into an opportunity for pow-wows. Inevitably, the farms foundered in the agricultural depression of the 1920's as did most Oglala-owned ranches. The Great Depression of the 1930's also devastated the non-Indian farmers and ranchers.

Despite the difficulties of the twenties and thirties, many Oglala elders remember the period fondly. Some families worked in the fields of Rushville, Gordon, and Chadron, Nebraska. Many became hired hands on non-Indian ranches. After payday, families journeyed to off-reservation towns and cities. Many camped on the way to Rapid City where they spent a few days renewing acquaintances. Several off-reservation towns made camping areas available to the travellers. Family trips to the Black Hills for herb gathering were part of the "good old days" too.

As often happens, American Indian policy changed again. In 1934, Congress approved the Indian Reorganization Act which permitted tribes to write constitutions. Of equal importance, the Bureau of Indian affairs officially stopped trying to suppress all Indian languages and cultures. The Oglala Sioux tribe agreed to a constitution drafted and supported by the BIA in 1936.

In the 1950's, America changed Indian policy again. Termination became the goal of the BIA and Congress, and Indians were encouraged to leave the poverty of reservations for a "better" life in the cities. Relocation programs paid for transportation, vocational training, and housing for entire families. Oglala families moved to Los Angeles, San Francisco, Milwaukee, and Denver. Some relocatees prospered, but most found urban poverty less desirable than reservation poverty. On the reservation, family support was available, and most Pine Ridge emigreés eventually returned.

In the 1950's, Congress withdrew the law which forbade the sale of alcohol to Indians anywhere in the United States. Unfortunately, the laws had not been effectively enforced even during the Prohibition Era. Oglala use of alcohol began during the fur trade period. Excessive use of alcohol has characterized much of American history, and the Oglala are no exception. Neither traditional Lakota government nor BIA officials were able to control the problems of alcohol abuse.

Perhaps the major reason for the continuing abuse is the bleak nature of Pine Ridge life for far too many Oglala. After the reservations were created, Indian males had no real function. Government programs promoted dependency. Paternalistic attitudes to even "successful" Indians promoted powerlessness as Oglala made no real decisions. By the 1980's alcoholism appeared to be waning, but the Oglala are left with its legacies. Most arrests on the reservation are alcohol related, most incidents of violence on the reservation are alcohol related, and many children's problems are alcohol related. Numerous reservation deaths can be attributed to alcohol.

Even at its worst alcohol abuse did not include most Oglala, and many consistently campaigned against alcohol use. The sale of alcohol on Pine Ridge Reservation remains illegal despite several referenda on legalization. During the past decade, public opinion has turned more and more against alcohol use, and Oglala leaders are seizing an opportunity to create programs to deal with the problem. Project Recovery for adults and Project Phoenix for adolescents combine mainstream techniques with Oglala cultural sanctions. Other programs include Alcoholics Anonymous chapters, Al-Anon, Alateen, and Oglala Lakota College educational programs.

THE CONTEMPORARY RESERVATION

The 1934 Indian Reorganization Act provided the Oglala with the appearance of self-government. The reality was that the Bureau of Indian Affairs controlled all meaningful activity on the reservation until the late 1960's. More than ninety per cent of the funds for the reservation were directly distributed by the BIA. Even tribal ordinances had to be approved by the Pine Ridge Agency Superintendent.

In the 1960's, the United States, inspired by President Kennedy and led by President Johnson, changed the face of America by recognizing the reality that many Americans were neither prosperous nor able to enjoy the political advantages of the dominant Anglo-American society. Civil rights legislation that guaranteed voting rights and the economic legislation of the Great Society changed Indian country and Pine Ridge Reservation forever. On

Pine Ridge Reservation, the chief importance of the Great Society and the growing American acceptance of cultural pluralism was that the Bureau of Indian Affairs lost its absolute control over tribal affairs. In a relatively short period (ca. 1965 - 1975), the tribal government budget went from less than $100,000 to more than $6,000,000 dollars annually. These funds meant that the Oglala could now actually determine their own government policies, direct their reaction to the dominant culture, and attempt to solve their own economic and social problems. The Bureau of Indian Affairs ceased to be the sole source of power and employment on the reservation. The Office of Economic Opportunity with its Community Action Programs insisted that all federal funds earmarked for the disadvantaged must have significant community control; this meant Oglala, not BIA control.

Reform administrations like those of tribal presidents Gerald One Feather and Al Trimble sought to return to a government consistent with pre-reservation Oglala political culture. This meant emphasizing the people of the districts and distributing governmental patronage to the districts. The decentralization effort included bringing in VISTA volunteers to assist in community development, importing college programs to train Oglala leaders, and increasing direct access to federal programs in Washington, D.C. Anti-Indian prejudices in border towns were to be met resolutely with economic and political pressure. Lakota language and culture were the hallmarks of the reformers. Many of the reformers identified themselves with those who had struggled to maintain Lakota cultural practices like Frank Fools Crow, a holy man from the Medicine Root District.

Those who had benefited most from the rule of the Bureau of Indian Affairs and its centralization of reservation programs in Pine Ridge Village became known as the conservatives. As the faction in power, they argued that continued centralization was the best way to modernize the Pine Ridge economy and benefit the people. They advocated continuing the BIA-style government, but with elected Oglala forming the government. In contrast, the reformers felt the weakening of BIA control provided new opportunities for the reservation and its people to create a government consistent with Lakota traditional culture. As always, the Oglala internal struggle over means and ends was influenced by external forces. During the 1960's, a militant Indian organization emerged among urban Indians. The American

Indian Movement (AIM) used techniques to defend Indian rights similar to those used by militant black organizations. Many AIM members travelled between Pine Ridge Reservation and cities like Los Angeles, Minneapolis, and Chicago.

Antagonism between the reformers and the conservatives grew steadily and was brought to the point of explosion by the murder of Raymond Yellow Thunder and others in border towns. The Oglala became increasingly polarized as tension built between the two groups. When Richard Wilson, a conservative, was elected President in 1972, succeeding Gerald One Feather, a reformer, the struggles occasionally turned violent as supporters of each side attacked each other physically. The Bureau of Indian Affairs was accused of using its police to assist Wilson's supporters. Eventually AIM entered the turmoil, as many AIM leaders, including Russell Means, were Oglala, and reformers asked for AIM to come. After a large community protest meeting in 1973, the community of Wounded Knee was occupied by numerous reform group members. Americans who formed ties to AIM during civil rights struggles arrived to help. The Federal government sent U.S. marshals and FBI agents to help the BIA and the tribal government control this challenge to the established government. All of Pine Ridge Reservation became an armed camp, and gun battles were common. Non-Indians on and off the reservation also armed themselves for protection. Television cameras and newspaper reporters offered assessments to national audiences, and many Oglala leaders sought out media attention. The reformers were united by their support of those in the Wounded Knee siege, and "Wounded Knee II" became a rallying cry. For many Lakota, the memory of Wounded Knee II is one of a courageous stand by those seeking self-government and defense of the Lakota culture against the federal government. For others, the siege at Wounded Knee demonstrates how radicals can destroy and cause chaos. In many ways, the division of opinions on the reservation reflects similar divisions in the larger American society that were fostered by the Civil Rights struggles of the 1960's. Today, the ideology of the reformers is widely accepted throughout the Oglala nation.

After the siege ended, it took several years for the bitterness between the groups to subside. Wilson was re-elected over Russell Means in a contest that even the BIA considered corrupt, but the polarization steadily decreased.

AIM members moved to assert Lakota rights to the Black Hills, were elected to the tribal council, and helped start a radio station- KILI. Many contemporary AIM sympathizers have joined former conservatives in community action programs which have greatly helped the reservation people. Some radical Oglala have joined in various efforts to regain stolen lands and have been responsible for continued confrontations.

In 1975, Congress completed the logical progression of efforts to implement self-government for Indian reservations. The Indian Self-Determination and Education Assistance Act granted tribes the right to contract to run Bureau of Indian Affairs programs for themselves. For instance, the BIA police force is now the Oglala Sioux Tribal police force. Its policies, procedures, and hiring practices are the creation of the Oglala Sioux Tribe's elected Public Safety Commission.

Reservation communities moved quickly to regain control of education from the BIA by contracting to operate several of the Bureau of Indian Affairs schools. Little Wound (K-12) in Kyle, Crazy Horse (K-12) in Wanblee, Lone Man (K-8) in Oglala, Porcupine Day School (K-8) in Porcupine, and Manderson's school (K-8) have all been contracted by their communities. Locally elected school boards provide policy leadership under the terms of BIA contracts.

Currently there is no significant conservative block that advocates a return to reservation politics of the early 1970's. The bulk of the Oglala have gradually come to accept that the days of a centralized, agent-controlled government were not good for the Oglala people. Since 1975, American Indian policy has promoted greater power for tribal governments. A better educated Oglala people want more self-government and wish to be able to remain Lakota, not assimilated Indians. Disagreement over means continues, but goals are essentially shared: preservation of Oglala culture, support for district governments as a means to restore community decision-making, consistent resistance to state and federal efforts to restrict Oglala self-determination, insistence on the return of the Black Hills, and persistence in reminding the federal government of its duty to meet its trust responsibility.

Though broad agreement on ideas exists, occasional squabbles and policy disagreements occur within the reservation. These disputes often reach the non-Indian news media and are reported as factionalism, feuds, and corruption, as if suggesting that Indian political life is somehow different from politics as practiced in the larger American society.

Despite general ideological unity, the most visible aspect of Pine Ridge Reservation is the poverty of its people and communities. There are numerous reasons for this poverty. Pine Ridge has few resources which can serve as the basis of economic development. Most farm and ranch land is not operated by Oglala because few have ever had the necessary capital– leasing remains their only option. The difficulties of farming are exacerbated by the practice of land inheritance by multiple descendents - one of the authors, for instance, owns 4/363 of a section of land. The reservation government, sometimes assisted by the BIA, has tried to encourage businesses. In 1990 only one industry, a uniform factory in Pine Ridge Village, employed more than a few Oglala. Pine Ridge Village also has a large grocery store from which the tribe derives income, and the tribe operates the Cedar Pass Lodge, a successful restaurant-souvenir-motel business near the Ben Reifel Visitor Center in Badlands National Park. These operations, and a few "Mom and Pop" businesses, constitute the private sector for the reservation. Other

Operated under a concession contract from the National Park Service, the Cedar Pass Lodge is a highly successful tribal enterprise. Photo by Dale Jensen, Rushmore Photo.

efforts, including a meat-packing plant, a tribal collective farm, and a moccasin factory have failed in recent years. These ventures were hampered by federal and tribal regulations and the lack of a skilled workforce. Few Oglala have been able to gain the expertise to operate businesses.

Most employed Oglala work for service agencies. The schools, social services, the BIA, the tribal government, and chartered organizations provide hundreds of jobs. Ironically, all of these jobs are tied to federal funding, even the state operated programs.

The tribal government collects a share of sales taxes paid on the reservation, receives indirect costs for operating several federal programs, and is paid lease money for tribal lands. The tribe attempted to pass an income tax in 1984 but the Bureau of Indian Affairs and Indian Health Service refused to cooperate. The Tribe's inability to exercise its sovereign rights has been crippling to reservation development.

Natural resources like coal and oil either do not exist or are too expensive to develop. In the past few years some interest has been shown in the development of zeolites in the northern Badlands portion of the reservation. Some groups on the reservation adamantly oppose such development as culturally unacceptable. All Oglala are concerned about the impact of mining on the environment, and there is fear that exploitation by outside companies could be disastrous - many have seen Appalachia.

Some economic opportunity exists in the area of tourism as many non-Indians have a great curiousity about the Lakota people. However, development of a tourism industry remains difficult because of the genuine opposition of many Oglala to what they feel is further cultural exploitation by non-Lakota. There are also problems of a lack of tourist facilities and a shortage of capital. Recently, the tribal government created an office of tourism.

Poverty brings other problems which are well known. The reservation population suffers from a high degree of alcoholism and substance abuse. This, in turn, leads to problems in the overall level of health, increased Fetal Alcohol Syndrome, assaults, and diet-related health problems. Cultural practices do not inhibit the spread of sexually transmitted diseases. Poverty is accompanied by a high rate of high school drop-outs (approximately 50% of high school age children are not in school), single-parent households, and self-destructive behavior. In 1990, NBC Television was awarded an Emmy for its descriptive series, "The Tragedy of Pine Ridge," a gloomy, negative portrayal of reservation life.

None could disagree with the facts presented, but NBC and most other media emphasize only the problems while ignoring positive aspects of reservation life. In the 1980's, numerous programs made an impact on the reservation's social problems. Through a combination of grass-roots and federally funded programs, the Oglala are improving the reservation through the same types of activities pursued in many other American communities. One difference on Pine Ridge Reservation is that many of the programs operate from a Lakota cultural basis. These include the Gray Eagle Society (tribal elders) and the White Buffalo Calf Woman's Society. Even the rebirth of Lakota religious practices has had an impact on the negative aspects of tribal existence because many ceremonies require abstinence and purification. At least a dozen Sun Dances are held annually on Pine Ridge Reservation. Most important, all of these programs, particularly those based on religious practices, legitimize avoidance of alcohol and drugs. Increasingly, the ill effects of poverty are described as controllable through community and individual action.

The Tribe recognizes the need to provide leadership and chartered Oglala Lakota College in 1971. The college provides an education for about 1000 students each year with a culturally sensitive Lakota curriculum. Oglala Lakota College is fully accredited and acts as a catalyst for tribal members and programs. Non-Indians take advantage of the academic opportunity as well.

Despite ample justification for bitterness, the Oglala generally are proud Americans. Armed services veterans always lead the dancers into a Pow Wow. More than 100 Oglala served in Operation Desert Storm in 1991. Even the Christian churches have continued to receive support from Oglala people especially since most have accepted the validity of Oglala culture and language. Most Oglala have no difficulty in maintaining membership in two religions– Christian and Lakota. There are Catholic, Episcopal, Presbyterian, Baptist, Mormon, Jehovah's Witnesses, and other congregations on the reservation, as well as those of the eclectic Native American Church.

Piya Wiconi, the administrative building of Oglala Lakota College. The College was chartered by the tribal government in 1971.

TOURISTS AND THE RESERVATION

Visitors are welcome on Pine Ridge. Although few of the amenities which tourists expect are available, a trip through the reservation is well worth the time. Pine Ridge's rolling hills and badlands provide scenery on a par with anywhere in South Dakota, and the reservation offers the added attraction of a society few Americans see. There are a few suggestions which tourists should consider. Pine Ridge Reservation is where people live; it is not a tourist attraction where people are paid to "act Indian." If you follow the Golden Rule, you will have a rewarding experience. For instance, you can hear the Lakota language spoken almost anywhere but don't stare or demand that someone say something "in Indian." If you want to take pictures of Pine Ridge residents, ask permission as you would expect in your own neighborhood.

You are welcome at the college centers, at pow-wows, at the tribal government offices and anywhere else. The only place you should not go unless you are invited is to one of the many Sun Dances held on the Reservation. Sun Dances are a particularly sacred ceremony, and many Oglala are uncomfortable when non-believers are present. If you should see a place where a Sun Dance is in progress, there will be gate keepers who will tell you whether you may attend. No pictures will be allowed, and you should not intrude, any more than you would want disruptions during one of your religious ceremonies. Always remember that courtesy includes respect for others.

There are numerous activities on the reservation. Pow-wows are held in nearly all of the reservation districts from June through August. At a pow-wow, you can see traditional Lakota dancing, Give-Aways, and Naming ceremonies. They usually begin on Friday nights and end on Sundays. Often, other events like softball tournaments, road races, rodeos, and parades are held simultaneously. The Oglala Nation Pow-Wow in late August is the largest and is held in Pine Ridge Village. If you wish to see a small, more traditional pow-wow, the Kyle Fair in mid-August is one of several held each year.

The Oglala Sioux tribal offices are located in Pine Ridge Village. The BIA agency offices, tribal court building and public safety headquarters are located in the same area. You are welcome to visit any of these buildings. Please remember that people work here, and there are no guided tours.

The Red Cloud Indian School and Heritage Center located north of Pine Ridge Village on Highway 18 is the former Holy Rosary Mission. It features a beautiful chapel, a school, and an art museum open throughout the year. There are Lakota crafts made locally which are available at reasonable prices. Usually, the Heritage Center curator can tell you who made the items. Lakota-made goods are available at the Cedar Pass Lodge in Badlands National Park as well. The Lodge is operated by the Oglala Sioux Tribe under a concession contract with the National Park Service. Most stores on the reservation carry Lakota-made items as well.

The Black Pipe State Bank, located in Martin on Highway 18, has a large collection of Lakota art, crafts and some non-Indian displays. This is privately owned but open to the public during banking hours. Martin has several motels and a shopping center. It is also the county seat for Bennett County, and its features are indicative of a bordertown community. Martin's population is about fifty per cent Indian. More information is available at the

Pow-wows are important cultural events. Heritage Museum collection.

tribal government offices. The tribe established an Office of Tourism in 1991.

One question visitors often ask is how much Oglala culture survives today. Of course, they mean how much pre-reservation culture remains identifiable. The two most obvious continuations are the Lakota language and pow-wows. Various medicine men hold sweat lodges and other ceremonies somewhere on the reservation just about daily. There are many Sun Dances beginning about mid-June and continuing through August. Many of the district or community pow-wows feature Give-Aways, which are the public expression of some ceremonies. Visitors may see Naming and Making of Relatives ceremonies too. Please remember to act as you would at your own ceremonies and do as other observers do. A casual visitor is unlikely to see a Vision Quest as these are essentially private. Keeping of the Spirit ceremonies are not open to outsiders either. Both ceremonies are common.

It is important for visitors to realize that Oglala hospitality is non-obtrusive. In Oglala culture one does not automatically talk to strangers. If strangers need something, they should wait for their turn to talk and then ask their question. If visitors are polite, they are welcome.

RECOMMENDED READING IN LAKOTA HISTORY AND CULTURE

There are numerous excellent studies of the Lakota. This list is by no means exhaustive. The authors suggest you start with the following:

Lakota History:

Hamilton, Henry W. and Jean Tyree Hamilton, The Sioux of the Rosebud, A History in Pictures. Photographs by John A. Anderson. Norman, Oklahoma: University of Oklahoma Press, 1971.

Sandoz, Mari, Crazy Horse: The Strange Man of the Oglalas. Lincoln, Nebraska: University of Nebraska Press, 1942.

Utley, Robert M., The Last Days of the Sioux Nation. New Haven, Connecticut: Yale University Press, 1963.

Lakota Culture:

Black Elk, The Sacred Pipe. Joseph Epes Brown, ed. New York: Penguin Books, 1971.

De Maille, Raymond and Douglas Parks, Sioux Indian Religion. Norman, Oklahoma: University of Oklahoma Press, 1971.

Mails, Thomas, Sundancing at Rosebud and Pine Ridge. Sioux Falls, South Dakota: Augustana College Center for Western Studies, 1978.

Stolzman, William, How to Take Part in Lakota Ceremonies. Pine Ridge, South Dakota: Heritage Center, rev. ed., 1988.